Not so
fresh prince

A book that is changing the game for entrepreneurs!

By **Johnny Macarter**

<u>Special thanks</u>

You will meet 10's of thousands of people in your lifetime but there will be a handful that really make an impact on your life. When you meet good people you hold on to them and you are always gentle with them.

I would like to thank Tracy D. for giving me an opportunity of a lifetime. Thank you for all your love and support in one of my darkest times. I am forever grateful that god put you in my life.

Alie, Thank you for believing in me, thank you for never letting me give up or underestimate myself. Thank you for riding this crazy wave with me. Thank you for being my soundboard. Thank you for simply being there when most weren't. Thank you for being, you.

Megan, thank you for being so supportive, so encouraging, so thoughtful. Thank you for being a listening ear, a fire under my butt when I needed it and simply being a good person and friend.

Sydney, thank you for being a good friend, thank you for giving me countless rides to ensure that I completed the program. Thank you for always being so motivating and encouraging. I really appreciate it.

Zoooooe, Thank you for being your crazy wild self. Thank you for being a good friend and lending a hand when needed. Thank you for the support and encouraging words. Thank you for being you.

I would like to thank all of my educators from cosmetology school, you all were very influential and encouraging. Thank you Ms. Kendrick for answering all 1,000 of my questions lol

Last but not least, Mike; Thank you for always having my back, thanks for all of the encouraging words, thanks for not letting me give up on myself. Thank you for reassuring me that genuinely good people do exist. Thank you for being you and not letting the world change that. Always

Honestly, when I first started writing this book I did not know who I was writing to, I just knew I wanted to use my experiences to help others because no one helped me nurture my gift...but now I know; This book Is for anyone who was born into any type of economic disadvantage. Black, White, Latino, Indian etc. No, It is not your fault that you were born into the situation that you're in but what happens from this day forward is 120% your responsibility. I'm going to give you all the tools you need to take back control over your life. But don't think you're just going to read

my book and poof, your life will magically be better. It's going to take hard work, it's going to take a level of dedication that you didn't know you had in you, It's going to take everything you've got, no games. People make up so many excuses for why they aren 't successful and the truth is you don't want it as bad as you say you do, because if you did nothing would be able to stop you from reaching your goals. No excuses. No plan B's. Just Blood sweat and tears. So tell me again, how bad do you want to be successful!?

Ok, let's go!

Most people will say they wanted to start their own business because they hated their jobs. I honestly didn't realize how much I hated my job until after I had been gone for a few months. It's like how they say you don't realize how unhealthy a relationship is until it's over. The type of person that I am, I gravitated to like-minded people. So I loved the people that I associated with at work. That's why energy and vibes are so important. We unintentionally invite people into our lives. We are judged by our energy before we are ever approached.

But anyway, I had left my job mentally long before I left physically and I had not even realized it. I was mentally drained more than anything. That's a different level of exhaustion. While I was at work I was planning my escape. Lol I worked at a prison. I was doing my research and finding the right business that I wanted to start. Day after day thinking, should I go to nursing school? Should me and my friends start a lawn service? That was a very short thought though because I hate the heat. I even considered just putting in for a promotion at the prison. But I knew my time there was winding down & I knew I no longer wanted to help anyone else live their dream, I wanted to invest in one of my own.

I have always been the indecise friend that bounced around from job to job because no job seemed to fit me. I did like working at the prison at first, I felt like I was making a difference being able to be a mentor to some of the inmates. But outside of work the income just wasn't enough, even after me continuously hitting my max on overtime. I remember thinking to myself, I can't create generational wealth on this salary. So the initial plan was to find a way to make more money and not have to burn myself out at work. I continued searching.

One day my friend Alie, who is now one of my best friends (who will be mentioned a lot in this book) came over and was being nosey in my room went into my closet and she saw a mannequin head with a barely started wig on it. She asked "Do you know how to make wigs?" to which I responded "I'm not sure I've never finished one, it's just something I do when I get in a mood." she said "finish it, I want to see how it comes out". So I did and she said it was pretty good. I still wasn't sure because as a guy I didn't know much about wigs or hair. I just knew I have alway been a little interested. She then said "You're actually good at this you should make and sell wigs as a side hustle." So I started pondering the Idea for a few days. I then decided that it would be a good business move. But I didn't just want to jump right in and put all my eggs in one basket so soon so I said I would start my business with selling eyelashes because they are a small ticket item as we like to say. It just means they aren't expensive. So I started doing my research; make sure to do research. I don't care what you are investing in. Knowledge is power.

Once I had my logo drawn up and found the vendor I was going to use for my lashes and packaging, I placed my order. Don't worry I will go into detail on how to do it all, later. Once I received the lashes I took pictures and immediately started to market them on my social media accounts and to my friends who I knew wore eyelash extensions. To my surprise it went really well. I received a lot of support from everyone. The more knowledge and support I got the more I felt confident with investing more into the beauty industry.   So I took some of the earnings from my eyelashes and invested It back into my business and purchased hair so I could make a lace closure wig.

I made the wig and installed it on alie after hours of watching youtube tutorials of course lol I enjoyed the process and what attracted me to lace wigs in the first place is how you can make the install look like the persons natural hair and hairline. I was never into fancy styles too much. I love the natural looks. My next step was to look into cosmetology schools that I could attend but none of them fit into my schedule. I worked a rotating schedule so my days off changed every week. On top of that cosmetology school is a full time program. So there was no way I could go to school and still work at the prison. I started to feel defeated at first, I chose to keep my job because I had bills and responsibilities like every other adult lol (sigh)

But then Alie, who is a MUA by the way, called me randomly one day and said "Guess who just signed up for Cosmetology school??" so I responded "Who??" Insinuating that she would never have signed up without me. Lol But she said "Me!" she Is very spontaneous in that way so I Immediately asked "Are they still open?"

she said "yes" and 'I said let's go back up there". So I walked into the school and I loved the vibe and the way they had it decorated and I remember feeling a sense of belonging, a sense of assurance. Like this was where I was supposed to be. It was that "You'll know when you know" feeling. But I still wasn't convinced that I should quit my job.

So I'm sitting there listening to the lady tell me about the program and the awards they won and all of the advantages I would have simply from attending this school specifically and I heard a voice say "just do it", So I did. I'm not messing with you, that is 100% how that happened. As you continue to follow my journey you will see I'm a free spirit. The lady then asked me "What about your job?"

I then responded "I will just have to figure it out. She said "Well then, welcome aboard"

On the drive home me and Alie brainstormed ways I could keep my job and still go to school but there was absolutely no way; I had to quit. Soon after, I was talking to a coworker about my plans and they knew how that job had been affecting my mental health so they Informed me that I could take a short term leave of absence due to my depression. Which I really needed regardless. So I contacted the proper personnel to get that taken care of and once I was set I started school which was kinda prescribed by the doc. lol She said "while you are taking time off, go find out what makes you happy" so I did.

So, now that things were lining up I knew that potentially I would be leaving my job soon and would have very limited income. I then broke the lease on my apartment and sold everything that would not fit into storage. I just wanted to be prepared for whatever was coming. I had plans to move in with my mother while I was in school but when the time came she had to move out of her apartment for personal reasons. Next I asked a friend could I stay at his place for a few weeks to figure something out. He said it was ok. He lived an hour away from the school one way so I was driving 2 hours a day to/from school for about a month. Then he moved out of his apartment. How ironic, I know. We all have our go through, man. I then reached out to some friends and family. Some wanted me to pay rent and others simply told me to figure it out. Although currently I was still getting paid from the prison I didn't want to commit to a rent payment because I knew those checks were temporary. So I said you know what, they are right, this was my choice and this is my journey so I will figure it out.
So I started living in my car. It wasn't as bad as I thought it would be. I used to park in the Walmart parking lot, in the same parking spot every night when possible. This was the Walmart I had been coming to since I was a child so I guess that's why I felt comfortable sleeping there. I had a routine. I would wake up, Go into the

walmart, use the bathroom and freshen up, turn on a motivational speaker on youtube, go to krystals and get breakfast, Breakfast scrambler with no meat, they knew me as the no meat guy lol then I would go pick up Alie and we would head to school while i recite motivational speeches word for word.

She finally looked at me one day and said "That's crazy that you know these word for word" but I had to engrave those words in my brain to stay sane. I had to believe that everything was going to be ok, even in moments when I wasn't sure. I had to believe that even though I am sleeping in my car I am worthy of the manifestation of the dreams that I was chasing. I had to believe that even though I was sleeping in my car that people still cared about me. I couldn't let the current situation confirm what I already believed to be true, which was that I was alone in this world. But that's for another book. These were the thoughts going through my head constantly so I had to fill my mind with so much positivity that doubt couldn't begin to penetrate the walls of determination and prosperity that I had put up to get me through this journey. I knew It would get rough.
I knew it wouldn't be easy and going into it with that mindset helped me a lot. when you prepare yourself physically and mentally for what is to come you can't be blind sided or manipulated.

No one at school knew that I was living in my car, only Alie and maybe one or two other close friends. I didn't tell anyone, not because I was ashamed but because I didn't need anyone feeling sad for me or trying to tell me how to feel and putting negative thoughts in my head. Also I feel like I reached out to the people I expected to help and they didn't so I was done asking for help I told myself I only have about 8 more months of this program and then I can have my life back. And even with everything I had going on I was still there for my friends and was a shoulder many times offering advice to classmates when my whole world was upside down. That's just the kind of person I am. Always had a positive attitude and warm spirit for others. Always trying to help.

After a few months of sleeping in my car my motor blew. Why do you ask? Well mostly because I used to have the car on with the AC running most of the night. In my defence I took it to a mechanic and told them I noticed a leak and they told me the car was fine. Lol After the motor blew they said " Oh the leak was way under there, we didn't see it" I simply said "Ok". That's where I'm at in my life, I choose peace. Every day.
I was on the interstate when the motor blew in my car so I had it towed back to the mechanic. I went and hung out with alie for a little bit and then I came back and slept in my car that night so I could be there when the shop opened in the morning. That's when they basically told me they missed the leak. The following night I stayed with Alie at her boyfriend's house. I know there are people wondering why couldn't you stay with your best friend!? For the record she was TOTALLY against me sleeping in the car and said she would sleep in there with

me if that were the case. And I told her no that is crazy I would be fine it's not that bad.

After the first night, when Alie's boyfriend realized I was going to go back and sleep in my car again at the mechanic shop, he asked the person he was living with if I could stay the night because I was sleeping in my car and she said "I just sat here and talked to him for almost an hour and he said nothing about sleeping in his car. He responded " Yeah that's the kind of person he is he doesn't like to ask for help or inconvenience anyone" so she called me back into the house and sat me down and basically told me that she asked her son and Alie and him about me and everyone speaks highly of me and after talking to me she feels like im a good person. She went on to say that I could stay there until I finished school and If I needed to and If I needed anything to just ask.

I ended up staying there until I finished school and passed my state boards test. She made me feel at home and was very helpful and still is. She's definitely like a second mom to me. I don't know if she knows but I tell everyone she's my god mom because god brought us together. I don't think I'll ever be able to adequately express how grateful I am for her. She even made sure I got to and from school some days. Some days I sat at the walmart across the street from the school because I didn't have a ride and she would still come get me after working all day.

When God places genuine people in your life, cherish them, this world can get very devious. I also made some amazing friends in school who gave me rides and saw to my well being. Lol I can honestly say that an experience that I expected to be one of the worst of my life turned out to be one of the best. I am very blessed.

In conclusion, I now work for myself full time. I'm not where I want to be but I have perfected my craft of lace wigs and I still have my own eyelash brand. I have added a Lace glue and lace protectors to my collection. I teach classes on how to perfect your craft on lace techniques and build your brand. I get to travel and do what I love. I'm also a life coach and I study human behavioural preferences. I use what has been coined as the DISC Assessment by William Marston many many moons ago. With this tool I can take you to a level you never imagined possible. Personally and professionally. My personal development skills know no limits.

I say all of that to say that if you really want something you have to be willing to sacrifice for it. You must stop at nothing to reach your goals. I once told my friend "I eat, sleep and breathe my brand. It's all I think about". You have to get to that level of determination if you want to be successful, If you want to create generational wealth for your kids and grandkids and so forth. You have to eliminate all distractions. Get off your phone, turn off netflix, the club scene isn't going anywhere, your friends will understand. And if they don't, tell them to buy my book. Lol You have to know, love and understand yourself before you can pour into another human being.

The sad truth is that we all fight battles we don't talk about, we all have bad habits to break. So let's uplift one another and be bosses together. This next section is going to give you all the info you need to get started on your boss journey. Are you ready?

Identify, Name and Register

The very first step is to identify what type of business you want to start. Ideally something that you enjoy doing and you do with the least amount of effort. That is called your gift. Statistics show that if you enjoy what you do it will hold your interest a lot longer. So don't just pick something because it is trending right now or something you seen someone else doing and it seems to be going well for them. Every business will be different because every business owner is different so there will be a lot of different factors that come into play here.

If you don't have a passion for what you are retailing once that trend fades away so will your ambition and soon your business will follow. But when you are passionate about what you do it doesn't matter what's in style or who's selling what because when you operate in your gift you will find ways to market, customize and retail your products because you don't want to have to stop doing what you are passionate about. That's why we all hate/hated our jobs because it wasn't what we were
Passionate about it was just a job to pay bills and we treated it that way but when it's yours, you're more gentle, you put your heart, body and soul into it.

So I'm here to tell you that if you
are not a "worker" you have other options and I'm about to
show you exactly how to do it.

So now we have to figure out what your brand
(Business) name will be. I say brand because you are
your brand 24 hours a day 365 days a year. The way you
carry yourself speaks for your brand. While this may
seem like a simple task but if you don't remember
anything else please remember that nothing about
success will be simple. This is a very time consuming
and strategic process; Longevity paired with ambition is
what conquers. When selecting a Brand name you
obviously don't want to use a name that is already being
used.
You don't want people confusing the two and miss
out on potential customers. I personally would stay away
from anything too vulgar or profane language just
because it's not professional and you don't want to limit
yourself on potential customers. You want to pick
something unique to you but relevant to your brand. I
Chose "Macarter Collection" because it has my name in
it and collection can be a vast variety of things it doesn't
limit me to one category. It is ok to google similar
business to get an idea of what is and is not appropriate.
No I'm not saying steal their name this is just to get you
brainstorming if you have no idea where to start because
the last thing you want is a name that is not cohesive to
yourbrand.
This is so important because your brand name
and your logo are going to be the first two things

potential customers see before going to your website or social media account. For example if you are a fashion stylist but your name sound like a hairstylist you will attract the wrong customers and you won't get a lot of clientele because it will be much harder for you to reach your desired client base. So I hope I have stressed how important detailing your brand name is and the same applies for your logo. If you are not sure where to go and get a logo made you can go to your local graphic designers which you can find on google, Instagram or Facebook. There are a lot of talented artists on Instagram and they are reasonable on pricing. For my local I recommend Icandydesignz LLC. They do all my work and their graphic designer is amazing.

Now you need to register your fictitious (Business) name.

Go to Sunbiz.org at least for my Florida residents. It may vary by
state.

Next you are going to click on "Start a business with E-file" then you will click on "Fictitious name registration"

then you will click on "Register a Florida fictitious name"

you may have to scroll down to it. And then you will just fill out the application with all the requested information.

After this is complete it will tell you that your name is registered and you are required to publish a new business advertisement in your local newspaper.

Now moving on to your business license, if
you are ready to do so you will need to call or visit your
local gross management office and inquire about the
requirement and steps for your specific business.

Some businesses require you to
have an office location and some such as a notary public
does not you would just use your home address.

Fees:
you are looking at about $150 for your business license
but it does vary
because if you rent an office space there are state
required
inspections that need to be done and approved on the
office
before you can open for business.

<u>Research and Customize</u>

Do your homework. What that means is you don't want to start a business in the blind or in and I will figure it out along the way, mindset. Yes there is so much you will learn along the way but and prior knowledge you can obtain will help
you greatly. You want to research other businesses in your area and in different areas to kind of get an idea of the business. Look up YouTube videos on it, the whole 9 yards. This is the best way to get tips and tricks on what work and what doesn't work, what's in demand and what isn't. What gimmicks may work and which ones may not. This in not to create competition
this is for you to get a feel of the business you are about to invest a lot of money into.

If you are a beauty influencer you
would look at other beauty influencers who do what you do preferably. If you plan to retail merchandise you would look at others who already retail that merchandise and just get some common knowledge of how it's done. Be sure to look up nearby
and far away areas because the lovely world of social media lets you reach people all over the world. Don't limit yourself, you want to be able to appeal to as many

people as possible. More people means more money for your business. Things to look for
are what's getting the most attention, what's not doing well and find out the "why?" You also want to see why the hotspots are hotspots compared to other places that are in the same market.

A good way to do that would be to look up reviews and see for yourself what the customers are saying. For example, Walmart is Notorious for not having enough registers open to accommodate its customers. So if I were to open up a grocery store one of the main things I would do is make sure that I always had an adequate amount of registers open to accommodate my customers to fill that gap. You always want
to find out what's missing in your field and fill that gap. That will always set you aside from other businesses. Two gaps that I noticed with selling eyelash extensions was that there was no consistency and not many people offered delivery so I filled those voids and it gains customer specifically because of those
things.

   I always have lashes on hand and I will deliver them to you or meet you to make it more convenient for you. Because what people don't realize is that your customers pay your bills so why not make them feel appreciated and respected. That's how you build a loyal customer and client base. Another thing to keep in mind also is that it's not always the best product that

gets the customer, it is the best customer service. That is why Everyone is raving about Chick-Fil-A lately. Customizing your business. When I started retailing my eyelashes I noticed that most people had simple lash boxes and they weren't customized. So I made sure my boxes were appealing to the eye and they have my logo right in the center. You can store your lashes in between uses and when you are tired of them and you are ready to get some new ones, what are you going to see with my logo? Having your logo on your boxes will
also help with promo because your brand will be floating around the city or the world and as more people see it the clientele will start to build itself. So definitely make sure your logo is neat and clearly printed on your merchandise no matter what it is. Do not, I repeat DO NOT get some cheap, poor quality logo or merchandise just to hurry and release your
brand. It will hurt you in the long run because your name is attached to that and professionalism is a key component in all of this.

Many people have told me that they purchase their lashes from me because they look so professional and I conduct myself and my business in a very professional manner. And that's something that I knew ahead of time. That's why I say this is a very strategic process. You always have to be a step
ahead of the game. You have to know the client base you want to target so you know who, what, where and why before it even happens. YES you need business cards. You won't always have a couple minutes to stop

and explain who you are, what you do and how people can get in contact with you or see your work.

So make sure all of that necessary information is on your business card. The biggest take away from this is you have to find out what is going to make your brand represent you and set you aside from others that do what you do. Do be afraid to give away free merchandise because if they like it they will shop
with you again and they will tell their friends and family about it. So make sure it's quality merchandise. Don't be afraid to do promotions and interact with your customers, be a real person not just the person behind the brand name. Make sure they know that they are not just a dollar sign to you.

Advertise and Marketing

This is probably the most important part because you can have the best merchandise in the world but if no one ever sees it that doesn't matter. So you want to advertise as much as possible. Talk about your business as much as possible to as many people as you can you never know who god will place in your path. You want to advertise every chance you get, post
about your business on all of your social media accounts a couple times EVERYDAY. Don't worry about people being tired of seeing your posts about your business. Because if they were tired of it they would delete you and at that point they weren't
doing anything but taking up space anyway.

Make room for true supporters. Every time I post something about my business at least one person shares it and that's all that matters. You also want to possibly reach out to and network with like-minded people. Look up networking events near you. You can
 plan everything on your own. A lot of people wait for someone to initiate the first step. We all know that a stranger is more likely to support you than most a lot of the people you know. It doesn't make sense to me either.

But what I do know is people who have nothing going for themselves are intimidated by people
potential and success.

Facebook and Instagram paid ads DO work I know because I use them all the time. I primarily use Instagram because that's where the beauty industry is right now. Paying to have your work advertised on social media is very smart and strategic. It allows you to reach thousands of people with minimal world from you leaving more time for you to perfect your brand. Also a lot of people don't know this but the owners of Facebook bought Instagram so if you pay for the promotion on Facebook and you have your Instagram linked it will promote on both sites for one price. Come on guys it's that easy. I know you all have heard the expression of killing two birds with one stone. Perfect example. Once again this is a very strategic process and it won't happen overnight.

You will put in a countless amount of hours and marketing and networking and may not get your desired results but rest assured that it will all pay off in the long run if you just stay consistent. You have to keep going because it's no doubt that your hard work is paying off and people are seeing your work. You just won't always get the satisfaction of knowing about it. That's ok because some days you will feel like you are on top of the world. So you take the good with the bad and you appreciate them both. Longevity and consistency wins the war. Will you be able to stand the test of time?

Find a vendor

Alibaba.com or download the app. They have thousands and thousands of wholesale vendors. Even if you are an influencer or someone who doesn't necessarily need their own merchandise. Go on this site and find you something to brand. Expanding your brand is never a bad idea. This site has anything
from household items to heavy machinery and because you are a business owner now you can purchase these things whole sale which means you get them at a much cheaper price than consumers.

In most cases you can have the vendor customize the merchandise with your logo to fit your brand. Some vendors will send you samples just depending on the vendor and the merchandise. I would recommend getting samples if you can just because you don't want to order 500 pieces of something, wait 2 weeks to get it because it's coming from China and it may not be what you wanted. Now you have to pay to send it back and go through that whole process again. So a huge piece of advice, don't say you have to merchandise until you physically have it in your possession.

Fortunately I never had a nightmare like that happen and I don't want you guys to go through that either so I'm giving you all the juice. When making a payment to the vendor make sure you are doing so on the website or the link that they send you takes you to the sight. Now because most of them are in china you will need to download "whatsapp" in your app store so you can communicate more effectively. The app also tell you what time it is where your vendor is located so that's a cool feature that I
liked when I was wondering why they were taking so long to respond. I also wanted to go over drop shipping very briefly for those people who may be interested in opening an online store. Drop shipping is when you find a vendor who offers drop shipping and you for a business relationship and your customers will place orders and pay with you but the merchandise will ship directly from the vendor. That will save you on startup costs because you won't have to make a bulk

purchase to make sure you have everything on hand for purchase and that eliminates needing all that space to store the merchandise and potentially being stuck and at a loss financially with merchandise that may not do so well at first. That first initial order is already a gamble unless you have thoroughly done your homework. Also download "Oberlo" this is a drop shipping website you can check out if you are still
interested. You definitely still want to do a lot more research on that because it is also very time

consuming. So get on YouTube and do your homework.

<u>Social Media</u>

I wanted to do a specific section on social media because rather we want to accept it or not this is the fastest way to reach the maximum number of people. So my people who have been in business for decades or more it's time to embrace the new era and new techniques. It will definitely help you out a lot. Running an EFFECTIVE social media account is a full time job which is why most if not all major companies hire someone
just to run that department. And they usually spend their whole work day on social media doing research and doing all the things I'm about to tell you about.

And it wasn't until I started doing my homework and researching hour after hour that I was able to find an effective strategy to advertise my own work and get over 1,000 profile views and over 11,000 impressions. Which is phenomenal when you don't have the followers to match. But what's crazy is I now realize the amount of time I spend on my phone on social media Networking, Promoting Yand Advertising. A lot of people don't think social media is a job or a marketing tool but I can tell you from experience it is both.

Instagram influencers can make up to$100,000.00 a year, depending on their following and that doesn't include brand deals and all the free merchandise they get sent that they can profit from. So yes this is a real job and you can make tons of money in it just remember it won't happen overnight. Longevity and consistency wins the war. Ok so I know you guys are ready for the rest of the juice on how to use social media and take your business or platform to the next level.
Do these things and you will do just that.

1. Go into your settings and switch to a business/Creator account. This will allow you to see how many people are watching and visiting your account, watching your videos, what city or state is your biggest following and when is and when isn't a good time for you to post. It will allow you to decipher between what kind of content your followers are most responsive to. This will also allow you access to pay for ads and it is the same on Facebook.

2. You want your page to have an esthetic, meaning you want your page to have a flow, you want it to look neat and be appealing to your customers. You want to stay away from randomly posting pictures. Also ideally you want to post good quality pictures; Remember professionalism is key. This is your brand invest in a better phone or a handheld camera of good quality. If you don't have a choice right now post what you have because you want to make sure you are posting content every day.

3. Captions do matter. You want your caption to be provocative in a good way. You want people to like and comment on your posts. A good rule of thumb is to post a question that people will engage in and respond to. That's what Instagram wants to see, you being active and you being social. Don't be afraid to comment on other people's posts or respond to your followers who comment on your posts either. Preferably people who are in the same field as you but if they are not it's not a big deal but following people who do what you do is smart because you know they are likely to be interested in your content. And you eventually build a big networking account. And that will also draw people to your page because people will see you commented on a mutual friends post now they want to know who you are it's that simple as well as you commenting on a complete strangers page. It creates constant traffic for your page. Same as if a stranger comments under your post the first thing you are going to do is click on their profile to see who they are and what they do. No different. You can't just sit back and wait for people to come to you. I'm from a small city I would never get any real traction.

4. Hashtags are soooo important. This is how you market
to your fans and potential customers. You want to use hashtags that are relevant to your business and even create your own hashtag. Not to many though because you want to use hashtags that a lot of people are

already following. Some people will say don't over use them and I agree but I also use a lot of hashtags and I haven't had an issue. Examples of relevant hashtags for me would be #Hairstylist and #OcalaHairstylist because you also want to tag cities and states when you use a broad hashtag like #Hairstylist. You also want to use hashtags from neighboring cities and states to wider your reach. For me an example would be #TampaHairstylist and #OrlandoHairstylist. Because I want to reach more people I also use #AtlantaHairstylist and #CaliHairstylist. Hashtags that I frequently use I have pre typed in my notes in my phone so I can just copy and paste and I don't spend 10 minutes inputting hashtags. You don't' want to only use those hashtags though you want to add more hashtags so you don't get flagged as a spam account. For example if I post a picture of a bob haircut I would use my pre typed template and them I would add #BobHaircut and #BobSeason. Now is it starting to sound like a job? This is how you get to the top of the algorithm, which dictates the order of which post appear in a persons newsfeed when they are scrolling and on the explore page. Hashtags are important guys.

If you have any questions feel free to shoot me a message on Instagram @OfficialMacarter or Facebook @Johnny Macarter

Join my text community and receive daily motivation and personal development tips. I also respond to personal

messages If anyone needs advice or just someone to talk to or brainstorm.
Text "Motivate" to 352-290-8759

How are you going to be your own boss?

____

____

____

____

____

____

____

____

What will your business name be?

What did you find in your research?

What are you selling/branding?

What strategies will you use to advertise?

____

____

____

____

____

____

____

____

____

Who is your target audience?

Do you need to go back to school?

What does it take to achieve your goal? Step by step

What are you willing to sacrifice to achieve this goal?

Do you need a coach or mentor?

Do you have a system to ensure your success? You need a system

How long will it take to achieve your goal?

Where do you pull your motivation from?

Who are you doing this for?
It has to be greater than you!

Now it's time to put your big boy/girl drawers on. Now it's time for personal accountability. Don't stop reading now, this is where it all starts to make sense. I'm going to give you an intro to what the flight assessment Is an how it's going to change your life forever.

Looking at this chart you will choose 2 words that best describe you. 1 of the 2 words vertically (Outgoing, Reserved) & 1 of the 2 words horizontally (Task,People). Once you have selected your 2 words you will find out which character/Letter you can mostly relate too. This does not mean that you are this character trait all the time in every aspect of your life. We exhibit all 4 character traits, but only 1 is your dominant preference. Your superpower

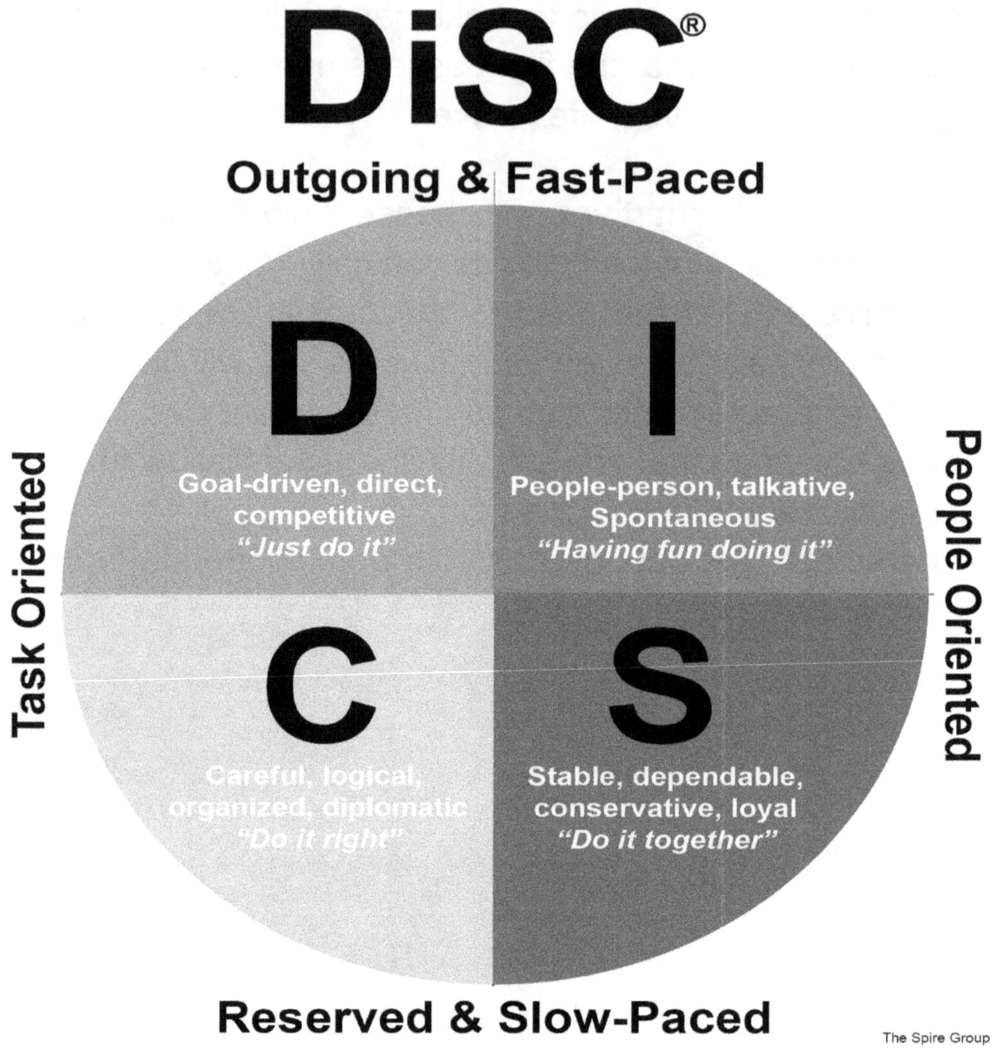

DiSC®
Outgoing & Fast-Paced
Task Oriented
People Oriented
D
Goal-driven, direct, competitive
"Just do it"
I
People-person, talkative, Spontaneous
"Having fun doing it"
C
Careful, logical, organized, diplomatic
"Do it right"
S
Stable, dependable, conservative, loyal
"Do it together"
Reserved & Slow-Paced
The Spire Group

If you are a *D*, this means people generally refer to you as Driven, Decisive, Determined, Aggressive, Specific and like to get straight to the point. You have also probably heard that you are a natural born leader. Authority figures probably left you in charge when they had to step away for a moment. This preference is Ideal for an entrepreneur but Don't get too ahead of yourself, even Michael Jordan needed a team.

If you are a *I,* you are probably often described as persuasive, enthusiastic, sociable, innovative and charming. You like being the center of attention most of the time. Very people oriented, emotionally connected & the life of the part. People love having you around because you make everyone laugh and make sure everyone is having a good time. The fresh prince was probably one of your favorite shows too because will was the best example of a "*I*" if there ever was one. He always kept the vibe going and everybody loved him. Oprah Winfrey would also be a good example of a "*I*" if you follow her.

Next is the **S**, Speaking as a fellow ***"S"*** myself we come off as somewhat shy, we are logical thinkers, we are consistent and reliable. We don't open up as easily as others, we have to establish credibility first. But all in all we are the glue that holds the team together. Always willing to lend a hand but doesn't want to be the center of attention.

Last but not least is **C**, These are the bill gates of the world. "***C***" can be described as cautious, analytical, and they are prone to having a system when making decisions. They are actually motivated by solving complex problems. They're usually not very talkative, a hardcore introvert. Lol

When you join my program & complete a short questionnaire, I will be able to go more into detail with you and speak directly to your superpower. We will be able to create a system that will not only align your goals with your daily activities but you will get answers to all those questions you have about yourself and why you do what you do. This system has been used in all aspects, personal, relationships, family and business.

If you are willing to do the work you CAN have the life you desire for not only yourself but for the generations to come. You just have to trust the process. Trust that hard work is rewarded. If you go on youtube and look up the success stories of some of your favorite celebrities like I said earlier you will see that they all had to invest hard work and dedication to get where they are. Everyone has their own journey but the principles are pretty much the same. Success comes at cost. Are you willing to put in the work?? Are you willing to sacrifice all the things the world has told you, you can't live without?? Are you ready to give it everything you've got?? ARE YOU READY TO BE SUCCESSFUL??

I'm the man that's going to get you there. Let's get to work!

Connect with me on Instagram @OfficialMacarter
Or text me @ 352-290-8759